The Therapy Process

From start to finish this process is all about YOU and YOUR needs. My Therapy Companion will walk you through how to make sure you are maximizing your process.

Discovery & Consultation

01

During Stage One you are working through the continuum of change and solidifying your decision to commit to the therapy process. You are soliciting support from a trained and experienced expert who will hold space with you along your journey. Although your selection of a therapist is paramount; always remember YOU ARE YOUR OWN EXPERT!!

Intake & Treatment Planning

02

Now that you have selected your therapist, Stage Two-the getting to know you phase- deepens. It is likely your therapist will need to capture a wholistic view of you as a person therefore you will have the opportunity to teach your therapist all about you via standardized paper assessments and live interview. Once there is an understanding of where you are now and where you'd like to be your therapist will assist you with creating goals that will guide the treatment process. This brief stage can be cathartic and maybe a little overwhelming but extremely important in ensuring your success.

Doing the Work

03

Your intake and treatment planning stage set the framework for how Stage Three will look. You've set the frequency at which you will meet with your therapist, the method for which treatment will be administered, everyone's responsibilities and what it will look like when "the work" has been accomplished. Now, it's time to roll up your sleeve, open yourself up to mindfully engaging the process while practicing new ways of being. You can totally do it!!

Discharge & Aftercare

04

Truth be told, Stage Four actually starts at Stage One (ie: always start with the end in mind) however your therapist will assist you will scheduling the actual end date for your time together and discuss how you will continue your therapy journey after this formal relationship ends.

STAGE ONE
Discovery
& CONULTATION

Things to consider during Stage One:

The question I am asked most frequently is do credentials matter? Yes and no. Yes, in that there is a degree of safety in choosing a certified, licensed and insured professional whose work is regulated by their licensure/certification board. There is safety in knowing the professional is held to a standard to include keeping up to date in the field, professional ethics and recourse if things were to go awry.

Even with these measures in place, there is never a guarantee that a professional will have mastered their craft or even have the chemistry you need to make your therapy experience successful. This is why I suggest your discovery process include knowing your needs, understanding your potential therapist's credentials along with an in person or virtual consultation to identify the therapist's "flavor". Choosing a professional therapist is much like choosing a spouse-choose wisely!

The American Psychological Association (APA) recognizes four different approaches to counseling: psychoanalysis, behavioral therapy, cognitive therapy, humanistic therapy in addition to a fifth approach which is considered an integrative or holistic therapy. It is important to note there are several interventions that fall under these wider categories. Each therapist may provide different interventions which you will need to discover during the consultation process.

These major approaches can further be divided into categories based on how information is processed during the therapy session.

TOP DOWN

Top-down approaches look to shift the way a client thinks – whether it's veering them away from unhelpful rumination or encouraging curiosity for their reactions. This approach is more talk based. Top-down approaches are helpful for individuals whom have a degree of mastery of their ability to self-regulate their emotions.

BOTTOM UP

Bottom-up approaches zero in on a client's raw emotions and defense systems by working with clients to calm their body down. This approach is more about connecting to the experiences in your body. It is helpful if you have struggled with allowing yourself to actually feel your feelings or if you have struggled with judging yourself when you do feel your feelings.

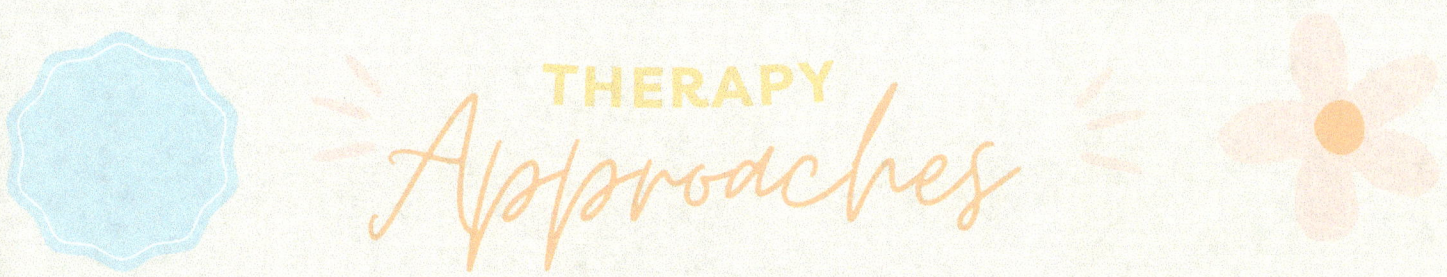

COGNITIVE THERAPY

Cognitive therapy is a short-term, goal-oriented therapy that focuses on the connection between your thoughts and your actions. It is intended to help change thought patterns that cause unhealthy or unproductive behavior.

What happens in sessions?

Cognitive therapy sessions utilize a top-down approach. A typical cognitive session may include exploratory talk exercises, skill building, going over what you did in previous sessions and discussing what progress you've made.

Is this approach for you?

Cognitive therapy works well for people suffering from anxiety, depression, stress, or phobias. It's also popular among people seeking to overcome harmful habits and addictions, such as smoking, overeating, or gambling. There is a strong homework component.

PSYCHODYNAMIC THERAPY

Psychodynamic therapy has a goal to help you acknowledge and understand negative feelings and repressed emotions so you can resolve internal psychological conflicts, and improve life experiences, self-esteem, and relationships.

What happens in sessions?

Psychodynamic sessions utilize a top-down approach. In a typical psychodynamic session the therapist will encourage you to talk freely about whatever is on you mind. The therapist will then assist you with making associations between what you are experiencing in your life and your unconscious thoughts.

Is this approach for you?

This approach is a popular treatment for people who are depressed. Psychodynamic therapy may sometimes be an effective short-term therapy but it often takes a year or longer to start to see the full benefit of sessions.

THERAPY
Approaches

BEHAVIOR THERAPY

Behavior therapy involves techniques used to change maladaptive responses to specific situations. It is said that altering the maladaptive responses can often alleviate psychological distress and psychiatric problems.

What happens in sessions?

Behavior therapy sessions mostly utilize a bottom-up approach. A typical session may include work on homework assignments, role-playing tasks, and practice coping skills. All of this is done through close collaboration between the you and your professional.

Is this approach for you?

Behavior therapy is used to treat a variety of mental conditions and is believed to be especially helpful for people with seemingly uncontrollable, intense negative emotions or those who may incline toward self-harm.

HUMANISTIC/EXPERIENTIAL THERAPY

Experiential therapy emphasizes you as a whole person, especially your positive behaviors and ability to grow, heal and find self-actualization through self-exploration.

What happens in sessions?

A typical experiential therapy session will help you explore feelings and experiences through creative interventions like guided re-enactments, role-playing and movement with the goal of raising your awareness of how and why you emotionally respond in any given situation.

Is this approach for you?

This approach is very client focused and thus non-directive which means sessions are less structured and based on the system of thinking that client knows best how to get their needs met.

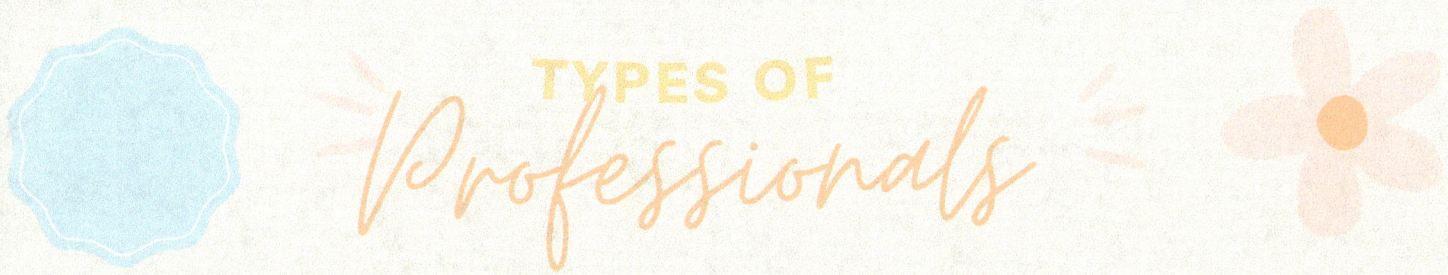

TYPES OF Professionals

PSYCHIATRISTS

Psychiatrists are medical doctors (M.D.s or D.O.s). As PHD level professionals they have the privilege of diagnosing and treating mental health conditions. They may assess, prescribe and oversee the use of mental health medication on routine basis.

PSYCHOLOGISTS

Psychologists have doctoral degrees (Ph.D. or Psy.D.) with specialized training in the area of mental health. Psychologists may work to help you gain clarity about your diagnosis and condition by providing standardized testing. They may also facilitate mental health therapy.

PSYCHIATRIC NURSES

Psychiatric nurses are registered nurses who work with mental health patients. Similar to a psychiatrist, they may assess, diagnose and oversee the use of mental health medication on a routine basis. The difference between a psychiatric nurse and a psychiatrist is that the psychiatric nurse has not completed medical school.

CLINICAL SOCIAL WORKERS

Clinical social workers are masters level professionals with specialized skills and training in the area of mental health. They are legally able to work with a wide range of clients and families which sets them apart from their other social worker peers. They typically have a strong foundation of client advocacy.

LICENSED COUNSELORS

Licensed counselors make up an array of masters level professionals who are governed by varying national bodies in the oversight of assessment, diagnosis and treatment of mental health clients. Among this group includes professionals such as: professional counselors, marriage and family therapists, sex therapists, drug counselors, clinical mental health counselors, etc.

NON-LICENSED COUNSELORS

Non-Licensed counselors make up an array of professionals who may or may not have training, certification but most importantly have not met licensure requirements in the counseling field. As such they are not governed by a licensure board. This may include pastoral, drug/alcohol, rehabilitation, etc.

Putting it together

WHICH THERAPY APPROACH INTERESTS ME MOST? WOULD I BENEFIT MOST FROM A TOP-DOWN OR BOTTOM-UP APPROACH?

WHICH TYPE OF PROFESSIONAL INTERESTS ME MOST?

Date : _____

Choosing to engage the therapy process can bring up a wide range of emotions. Bringing your awareness to what your thoughts and feelings about the process-including any pre-conceived notions you may hold- can be helpful in navigating the start to your healing journey. Take a moment to reflect on how you came to the decision to pursue therapy and where you are in the process today. Note these thoughts below.

"Do the best you can until you know better. Then when you know better, do better."

-Maya Angelou

Helpful Reminder:

Stay open minded during this process. Being able to change and revise outdated or incorrect beliefs is an important part of learning and personal growth.

Affirmation: I give myself permission to change my mind.

List your favorite affirmations

- _____
- _____
- _____

What are the most significant challenges noted in your journal entry?

How can therapy best support you in your journey?

Happy
SEARCHING

Now that you are clearer on your basic needs and types of therapy approaches, it is time to use this information to begin the daunting task of searching for your therapist. Below are helpful considerations for your search.

Brainstorm

- What kind of personality works best for you?
- Do you have a preference of gender?
- Do you want a therapist who has a similar background to you?
- Do you prefer virtual or in person sessions?
- What is your availability?
- How will you finance your services?

Resources

Below is a list of online resources to get you started. You will be able to filter your search by what is important to you such as gender, approach, location etc.

- **Psychology Today (psychologytoday.com)**
- **Therapy for Black Girls (therapyforblackgirls.com)**
- **Black Therapists Rock (blacktherapistsrock.com)**
- **Clinicians of Color (cliniciansofcolor.org)**
- **The Boris Lawrence Henson Foundation (borislhensonfoundation.org)**
- **The Loveland Foundation (thelovelandfoundation.org)**
- **Megan Thee Stallion Resource (badbitcheshavebaddaystoo.com)**
- **Therapy Den (therapyden.com)**
- **Therapy for Black Men (therapyforblackmen.org)**
- **Talk Space (talkspace.com)**
- **Mental Health America (mentalhealthamerica.net)**
- **National Alliance on Mental Illness nami.org**
- **Alcoholics Anonymous aa.org**
- **Narcotics Anonymous na.org**
- **National Suicide Prevention Lifeline, 1-800-273-TALK (8255),**

Connect

When you find a few potential therapists, reach out to them by email or by phone. Introduce yourself, see if they're accepting new patients and ask to set up a free 15 minute phone consultation. This is the risk free time to identify if there is chemistry between you and a potential therapist.

RESEARCH LOG

PROFESSIONAL'S NAME:

PHONE NUMBER:

ACCEPTING NEW PATIENTS: Y   N

WEBSITE:

SPECIALITY INDICATED:

WHAT INITIALLY DRAWS YOU TO THIS PERSON?

CONSULTATION SCHEDULED FOR:

PROFESSIONAL'S NAME:

PHONE NUMBER:

ACCEPTING NEW PATIENTS: Y   N

WEBSITE:

SPECIALITY INDICATED:

WHAT INITIALLY DRAWS YOU TO THIS PERSON?

CONSULTATION SCHEDULED FOR:

PROFESSIONAL'S NAME:

PHONE NUMBER:

ACCEPTING NEW PATIENTS: Y   N

WEBSITE:

SPECIALITY INDICATED:

WHAT INITIALLY DRAWS YOU TO THIS PERSON?

CONSULTATION SCHEDULED FOR:

RESEARCH LOG

PROFESSIONAL'S NAME:

PHONE NUMBER:

ACCEPTING NEW PATIENTS: Y   N

WEBSITE:

SPECIALITY INDICATED:

WHAT INITIALLY DRAWS YOU TO THIS PERSON?

CONSULTATION SCHEDULED FOR:

PROFESSIONAL'S NAME:

PHONE NUMBER:

ACCEPTING NEW PATIENTS: Y   N

WEBSITE:

SPECIALITY INDICATED:

WHAT INITIALLY DRAWS YOU TO THIS PERSON?

CONSULTATION SCHEDULED FOR:

PROFESSIONAL'S NAME:

PHONE NUMBER:

ACCEPTING NEW PATIENTS: Y   N

WEBSITE:

SPECIALITY INDICATED:

WHAT INITIALLY DRAWS YOU TO THIS PERSON?

CONSULTATION SCHEDULED FOR:

CONSULTATION LOG

Professional's name: | **Practice Name:**

Helpful questions to ask during your initial consultation

- What is your background?
- What is your approach to therapy?
- Are you licensed in my state?
- How long have you been practicing?
- Do you have experience working with my specific issues?
- How long are your sessions?
- Do you accept my insurance?
- What is your intake process like?

My initial impression:

Provider in my insurance network: Y   N

Cost for initial session:

Cost for follow up session:

My copay/deductible for this provider is:

Does provider offer sliding scale or EAP? Y N

Consultation Notes:

_____

_____

_____

_____

Action Items:

_____

_____

_____

_____

CONSULTATION LOG

Professional's name: **Practice Name:**

My initial impression:

Provider in my insurance network: Y   N

Cost for initial session:

Cost for follow up session:

My copay/deductible for this provider is:

Does provider offer sliding scale or EAP? Y N

Consultation Notes:

_____

_____

_____

_____

Action Items:

_____

_____

_____

_____

CONSULTATION LOG

Professional's name: **Practice Name:**

My initial impression:

Provider in my insurance network: Y   N

Cost for initial session:

Cost for follow up session:

My copay/deductible for this provider is:

Does provider offer sliding scale or EAP? Y   N

Consultation Notes:

_____

_____

_____

_____

Action Items:

_____

_____

_____

_____

STAGE TWO

Intake

& TREATMENT PLANNING

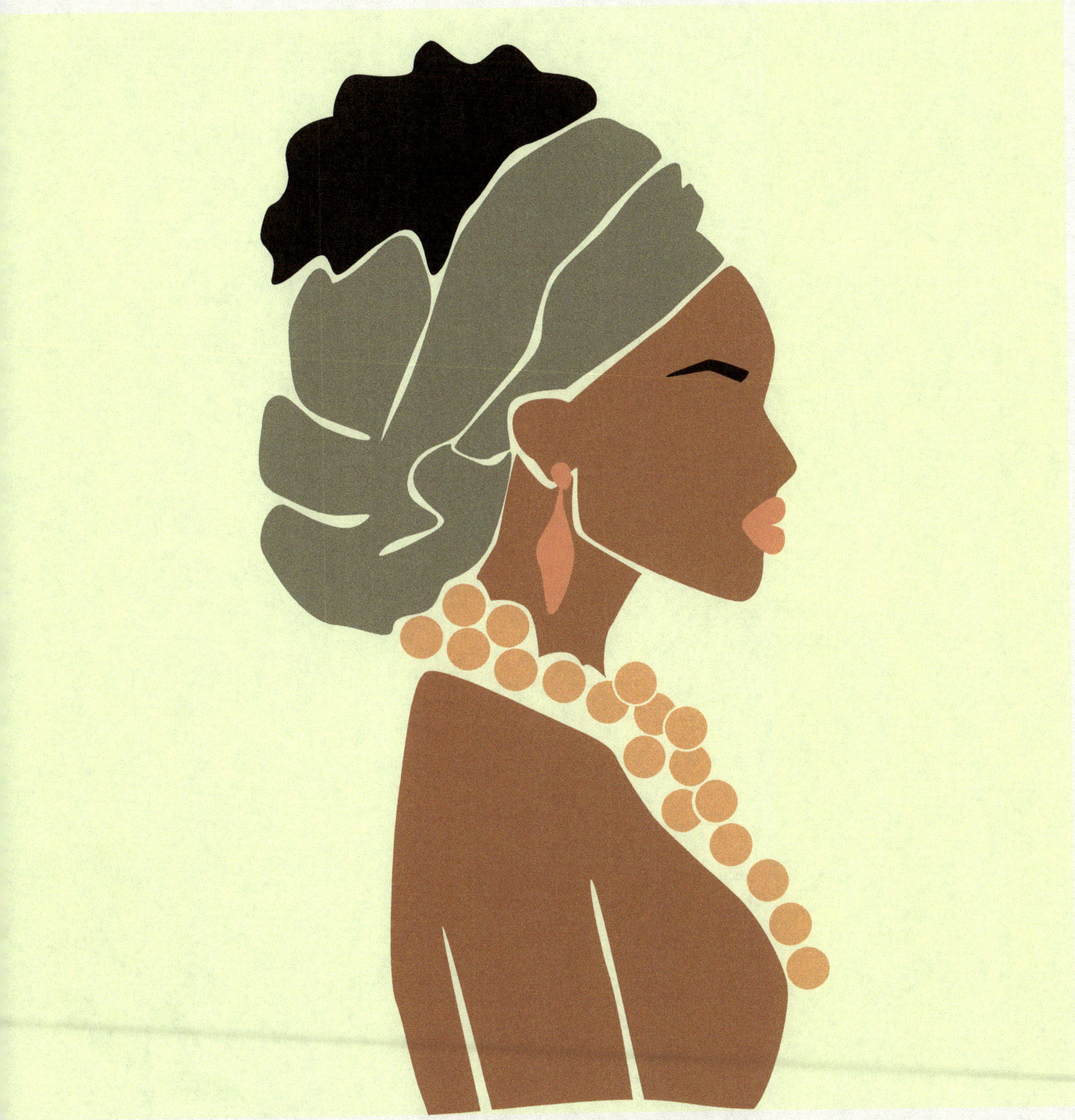

Dear
DIARY

You've made it through stage one-you have found YOUR person-your therapist! Now is a great time to assess what you are thinking and feeling about your therapy process. Any jitters, second thoughts, all out wanting to run? Dump it all below. You may even find it helpful to talk with your therapist about your apprehensions.

The Low Down

YOUR FIRST THERAPY SESSION IS A PRIME MOMENT THAT CATAPULTS YOUR BUDDING RELATIONSHIP WITH YOUR THERAPIST. IT IS DIFFERENT FROM ALL OTHER SESSIONS. IT IS AN OPPORTUNITY TO FURTHER EXPLORE MUTUAL CHEMISTRY WHILE BUILDING THE FOUNDATION FOR WHICH YOUR HEALING JOURNEY THRIVES.

DURING THE INITIAL SESSION YOUR THERAPIST GIVES YOU THE SKINNY ON HOW YOUR PROCESS WILL WORK, YOU SHARE-ON A DEEPER LEVEL-YOUR CONCERNS AND NEEDS AND YOUR THERAPIST GETS TO KNOW YOU.

ONE WAY YOUR THERAPIST GETS TO KNOW YOU IS THROUGH THE USE OF FORMS. THERE ARE PROBABLY GOING TO BE MANY OF THEM TO FILL OUT. THESE COULD INCLUDE INFORMED CONSENT, HIPAA RELATED, PRACTICE SPECIFIC FORMS, RELEASE OF INFORMATION, QUESTIONNAIRES AND/OR ASSESSMENTS ETC; SO BE READY TO REPEAT YOURSELF A LOT.

BEING HONEST WITH YOUR THERAPIST IS CRUCIAL. THERAPISTS KNOW HOW CHALLENGING IT CAN BE TO TALK ABOUT HARD THINGS YOU MAY HAVE EXPERIENCED BUT THEY ALSO KNOW HOW MUCH OF A NEED IT IS AND RELIEF IT FEELS TO GET IT OFF YOUR CHEST. ALTHOUGH GETTING IT ALL OUT DOESN'T HAPPEN WITHIN THE FIRST SESSION, IT DOES PREPARE YOU FOR THE DEEPER DIVE THAT WILL HAPPEN IN THE FORTHCOMING WEEKS.

Prepare!

ONCE YOU REACH OUT AND ARRANGE YOUR FIRST THERAPY SESSION, YOU'RE LIKELY TO FEEL NERVOUS OR SCARED, ESPECIALLY IF YOU'RE NEW TO THERAPY. AS YOUR FIRST APPOINTMENT NEARS, HERE ARE SOME WAYS TO MENTALLY AND PHYSICALLY PREPARE YOURSELF:

1

Before your first session, outline clear therapy goals for what you hope to achieve from counseling. There are no right or wrong reasons to seek therapy. Try to understand what brought you to therapy and how you hope to leave. It may be helpful to revisit your personal reflection completed in stage one of this companion.

2

Being open and honest about your thoughts and feelings is crucial if you want to get the most out of therapy. That doesn't mean you need to tell all your innermost feelings in the first session, but allow yourself to be a little more open while talking. Remember, the therapist isn't there to judge you, but rather to help you. Everything you say is completely confidential.

3

Be sure to schedule your session at a convenient time so you are not rushing to or from activities. It will be helpful that you are in a safe, comfortable, private location where you will be secure with disclosing your intimate details. Being well hydrated and satiated can be helpful to ensure you are up to the session tasks.

BE IN THE KNOW!

Your therapist will be assessing you. Being in the know means getting an idea of your assessment results so you can start considering what your treatment goals will be in the next stage.

Below is space to gather feedback from your therapist. Here's a hint: your therapist may not initiate this feedback session, so you may need to ask for it!

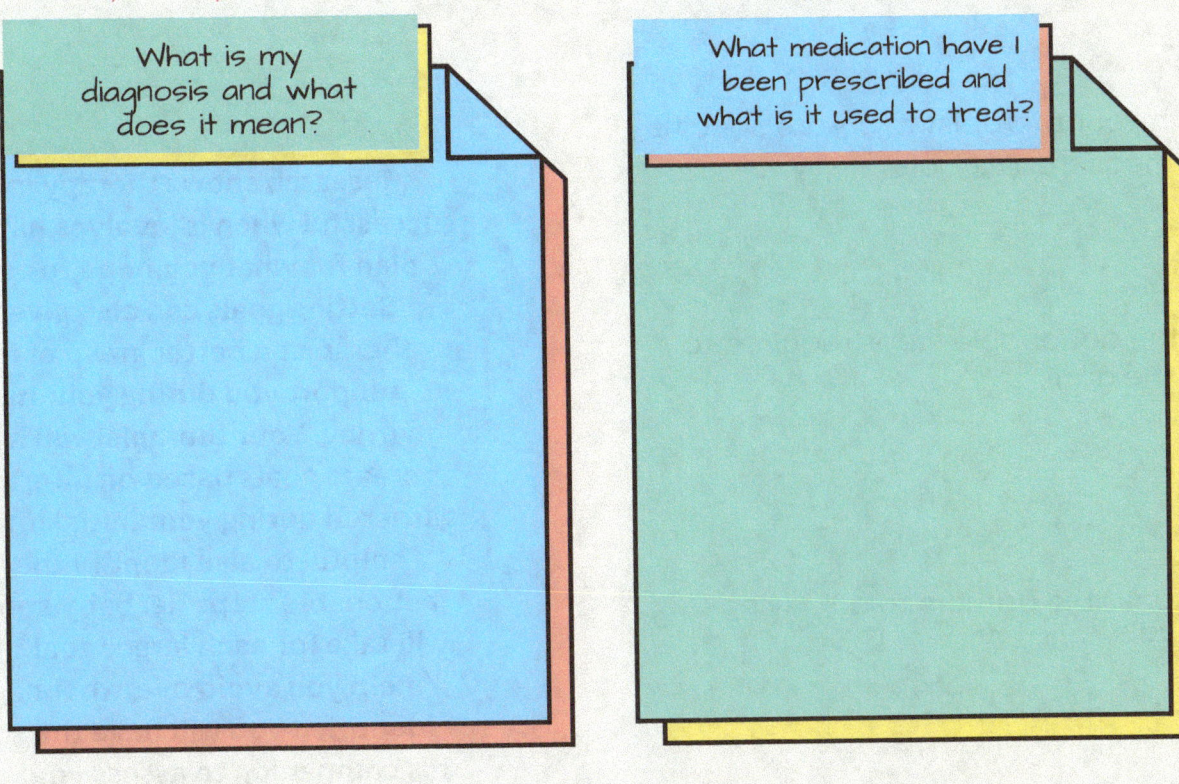

What is my diagnosis and what does it mean?

What medication have I been prescribed and what is it used to treat?

Which assessments have my therapist used and what are the results?

What are my therapist's clinical opinions of my case?

Sis got
GOALS

○ **Fully assess and articulate the problem**

When considering how your problem area shows up in your life you want to be able to quantify the observed intensity, duration and frequency of the unwanted issue. (ex: my anger is an 8/10, lasts 30 minutes, 6 days p/week.

○ **Work with your therapist to create specific, realistic measurable goals**

You want to know when you have accomplished the goal. Specific refers to exactly what you want to see; realistic refers to the goal being a natural extension or baby step to where you are currently; measurable refers to quantifying the goal.

○ **Identify the actionable steps required to achieve the goal.**

You'll avoid burnout by allowing your action steps to be challenging enough that they are out of your comfort zone but small enough to not overwhelm you by triggering your body's stress response system. If you find you're feeling overwhelmed, scale your goal back a tad bit until you feel safe again-wash and repeat. You will be gradually exposing yourself to "the new thing".

○ **Address possible barriers to achieving stated goals**

Every behavior, person, thing etc. serves a function in our lives. Taking a step back to non-judgmentally build awareness of that function and how it contributes to the unwanted experiences in our lives is a step toward extinguishing the impact any barrier has on our goal achievement.

○ **Frequently assess your progress and adjust as needed**

This process can definitely feel like an experiment. It is finding the courage to "try on" new skills to see how they fit with who you are and who you are becoming. Be patient with yourself in the fitting room; you'll get there. Give yourself permission to tailor your life to who you are at every stage of your life.

— goals —

Research shows therapy is more successful when it involves having a set plan for what you hope to achieve. Setting goals can also give your therapist a better grasp of how to support you during your healing journey. Your therapist will help you create goals based on information gathered during your initial intake. It is helpful to also identify the small actionable steps (ie: baby steps) you will take for each larger goal. This will help you avoid overwhelm. Once identified you will have the space in this companion to assess your progress monthly.

Values exploration

Dig Deeper

Values help us in our decision making process and therefore help to guide our lives. The more we choose our goals based on our values and principles, the more aligned and satisfied we will feel in our life. Use this section to brainstorm which values are influencing your treatment goals.

My Goals List
GOAL SETTING EXAMPLE

MONTH ONE DATE: OCTOBER 25, 2022

GOAL 1

EXAMPLE PROBLEM AREA: I FEEL SAD AND CAN'T GET OUT OF THE BED TO GO TO WORK

NOT SPECIFIC, MEASUREABLE AND/OR REALISTIC GOAL: I WILL FEEL HAPPY

SPECIFIC, MEASUREABLE AND/OR REALISTIC GOAL: I WILL IDENTIFY 3 CHARACTERISTICS OF HAPPINESS

GOAL 2

EXAMPLE PROBLEM AREA: I FEEL SAD AND CAN'T GET OUT OF THE BED TO GO TO WORK

NOT SPECIFIC, MEASUREABLE AND/OR REALISTIC GOAL: I WILL FEEL HAPPY

SPECIFIC, MEASUREABLE AND/OR REALISTIC GOAL: I WILL IDENTIFY 3 FACTORS THAT CONTRIBUTE TO MY POOR MOOD.

GOAL 3

EXAMPLE PROBLEM AREA: I FEEL SAD AND CAN'T GET OUT OF THE BED TO GO TO WORK

NOT SPECIFIC, MEASUREABLE AND/OR REALISTIC GOAL: I WILL FEEL HAPPY

SPECIFIC, MEASUREABLE AND/OR REALISTIC GOAL: I WILL GET OUT OF THE BED AND GO TO WORK 3 TIMES PER WEEK.

ACTIONS I NEED TO TAKE

DAILY I WILL SPEND 10 MINUTES REFLECTING ON WHAT PROMOTES FEELINGS OF HAPPINESS IN MYSELF

I WILL IDENTIFY THE BEST TIME FOR MY DAILY REFLECTION

I WILL CREATE BOUNDARIES WITH MY LOVED ONES TO ENCOURAGE MY PERSONAL TIME

ACTIONS I NEED TO TAKE

DAILY I WILL SPEND 10 MINUTES REFLECTING ON FACTORS THAT CONTRIBUTE TO MY POOR MOOD

I WILL IDENTIFY THE BEST TIME FOR MY DAILY REFLECTION

I WILL CREATE BOUNDARIES WITH MY LOVED ONES TO ENCOURAGE MY PERSONAL TIME

ACTIONS I NEED TO TAKE

DAILY I WILL SPEND 10 MINUTES REFLECTING ON FACTORS THAT CONTRIBUTE TO MY INABILITY TO GET OUT OF BED AND GO TO WORK

I WILL IDENTIFY THE BEST TIME FOR MY DAILY REFLECTION

I WILL CREATE BOUNDARIES WITH MY LOVED ONES TO ENCOURAGE MY PERSONAL TIME

 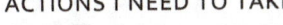

MONTHLY PROGRESS

THIS MONTH I EXPERIENCED DIFFICULTY CREATING BOUNDARIES WITH MY LOVED ONES AND WAS NOT CONSISTENT WITH PRIORITIZING MY PERSONAL TIME.

MONTHLY PROGRESS

THIS MONTH I WAS ABLE TO IDENTIFY FACTORS THAT CONTRIBUTE TO MY POOR MOOD. I DO NOT KNOW WHAT TO DO ABOUT THESE FACTORS AND NEED HELP WITH ADDRESSING THESE IDENTIFIED FACTORS.

MONTHLY PROGRESS

THIS MONTH I WAS ABLE TO IDENTIFY THAT I AM TIRED BECASUE OF THE MULTIPLE TASKS I COMPLETE. I HAVE A HARD TIME SAYING "NO" AND NEED TO CONTINUE WORKING ON THIS SO THAT I HAVE MORE TIME FOR MYSELF.

NOTES

CREATING MY GOALS MAKES ME FEEL HOPEFUL ABOUT MY HEALING JOURNEY. I LEARNED A LOT ABOUT MYSELF OVER THE LAST MONTH THAT I WANT TO CONTINUE WORKING ON. I NEED TO TALK TO SO MANY PEOPLE IN MY LIFE LIKE MY BOSS ABOUT MY WORKLOAD AND MY FAMILY. THIS IS HARD FOR ME AND MAY NEED TO GET SUPPORT FROM MY THERAPIST ABOUT THIS PART OF MY GOALS.

My Goals List
MONTH 1

MONTH ONE DATE:

GOAL 1

GOAL 2

GOAL 3

ACTIONS I NEED TO TAKE

ACTIONS I NEED TO TAKE

ACTIONS I NEED TO TAKE

WHAT CAN I TELL MYSELF IF THINGS GET HARD

WHAT CAN I TELL MYSELF IF THINGS GET HARD

WHAT CAN I TELL MYSELF IF THINGS GET HARD

NOTES

ADDRESSING BARRIERS
EXERCISE

1. Visualize Yourself without judgement

All human behaviors become strengthened by repetition then lived out unconsciously. It is helpful to bring conscious awareness back to how you live your life in order to identify the root of your barrier(s) to success. Visualizing yourself attempting a goal is a strategy to uncover hidden barrier(s).

Pick a problem area

Without judgement, see yourself attempting to accomplish the goal

What happens before, during and after?

2. Understand the Function

As you visualized yourself what did you identify as occurring before, during and after your goal directed effort? This is your clue to understanding your barrier/deeper needs.

To understand your barrier(s) you MUST! understand the purpose it serves.

The American Psychological Association has categorized the purpose of our behavior choices as indicated below. Consider if the behavior you chose unintentionally met a purpose indicated below?

- ☐ **Attention:** garnering awareness of a person to the exclusion of the person's other stimuli

- ☐ **Access to Tangibles:** behaviors intended to to assist us with gaining a thing we otherwise could not gain independently

- ☐ **Sensory Stimulation:** engaging in a pleasant experience in order to replace unpleasant experiences

- ☐ **Escape:** an attempt to move away from or eliminate a present but unwanted stimulus

3. Address with Grace

Now that you have a deeper understanding of what gets in the way of your intended goal it is time to extend yourself the necessary compassion which allows you the freedom to address your real need- whether those needs are addressed within yourself or with another person.

Below, brainstorm ways you may be able to address your real need(s) in a value consistent manner that actually works for you.

_____

_____

_____

_____

_____

_____

STAGE THREE

Doing

THE WORK!

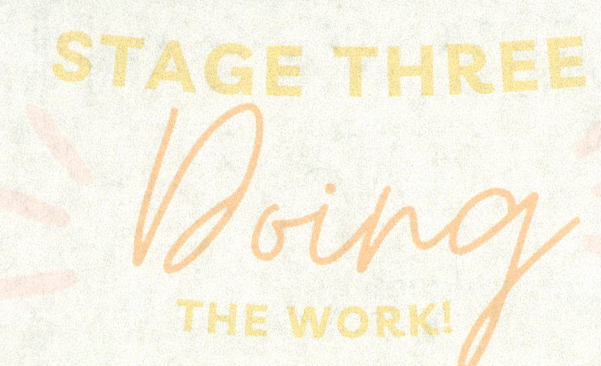

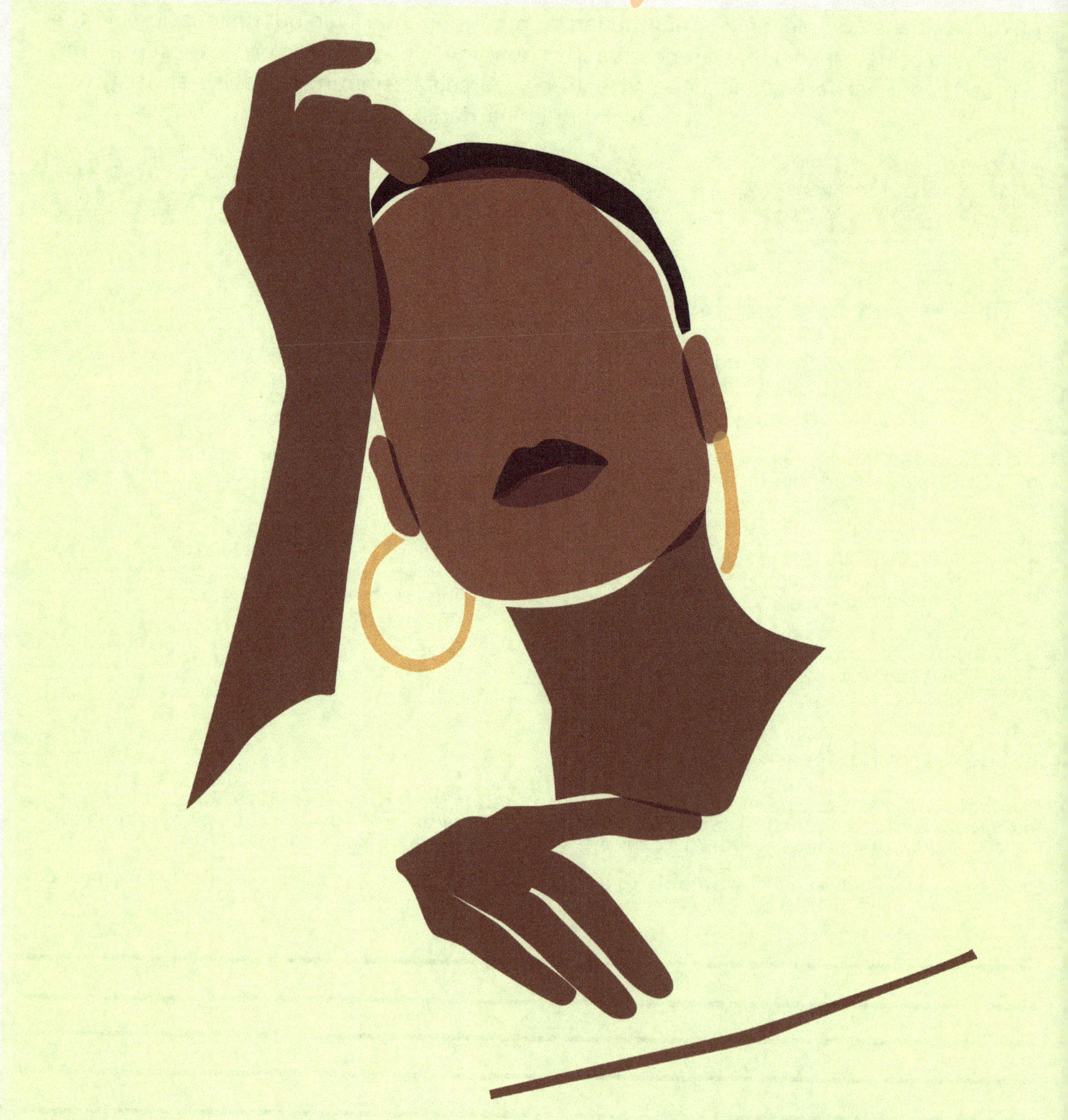

YOUR STRESS RESPONSE SYSTEM

Your body comes equipped with an emergency reaction system much like a fire alarm in a building. This stress response system is managed by your brain and helps you stay alive and safe in the face of external or internal (psychological) threats. When the stress response is turned on, your body may release chemicals that trigger the reactions indicated below by LifeStance Health.

Having an understanding of your response style can help you know when you need to create safety for yourself in order to encourage your treatment goals.

FIGHT

Unhealthy Fight Response:

Controlling behaviors
Narcissistic tendencies
Bullying
Conduct disorder
Demanding perfection from others
Feelings of entitlement

Healthy Fight Responses:

Create boundaries
Be assertive
Find courage
Become a strong leader
Protect yourself (and loved ones) when necessary

FLIGHT

Unhealthy Flight Response:

Obsessive or compulsive tendencies
Needing to stay busy at all times
Panic and constant fear
Perfectionism
Workaholic tendencies
An inability to sit still

Healthy Flight Responses:

Disengage from harmful conversations
Leave unhealthy relationships
Remove yourself from physically dangerous situations
Properly assess danger

FAWN

Unhealthy Fawn Response:

Codependent relationships
Someone to stay in a violent relationship
Loss of self
People-pleasing to the point of destruction
Little or no boundaries

Healthy Fawn Responses:

Compassion for others
Compromise
Active listening
Fairness

FREEZE

Unhealthy Freeze Response:

Dissociation
Isolation
Frequent "zoning out"
Brain fog
Difficulty making decisions or taking actions
Perceived laziness
Fear of achieving or trying new things

Healthy Freeze Responses:

Mindfulness
Awareness
Full presence in the moment

The Work
&
Self-Care

Doing the work refers to the process of addressing any self-defeating limitation interfering with you embodying the desired version of yourself. It is important to remember: shifting into wholeness is not a passive occurrence. Instead, it is awakening the courage within that allows you the freedom to advance into unfamiliar territories.

Because this work is so active, the practice of self-care naturally goes hand in hand with it. Self-care ensures your basic needs are met which helps you to feel safe enough to avoid triggering your body's natural stress response system previously discussed.

I have found most people believe they will feel great following a therapy session however this is not always the case. In fact, immediately following a session you may experience feeling: physically tired, emotionally drained, tearful, on edge and even irritable. While this is all a necessary part of your wholeness journey, it also amplifies the need for intentional self-care which is why it is advised to normalize this practice on a daily basis.

Below, brainstorm ways you can sustain psychological safety pre and post therapy session. If you have difficulty with developing ideas, I have included a self-care challenge you may find useful.

Also included are monthly self-care assessments and reflection questions. Feel free to notice how each month you become more attuned with your needs.

Physical Self-Care	Mental/emotional Self-Care

Spiritual Self-Care	Environmental Self-Care

Mood Tracker

Take a few days to notice which activities contribute to your overall mood (good or bad). Note your observations below along with the intensity of your experience (1-10 with 10 being the most intense). Your higher numbered activities may indicate a need for creating safety around the noted activity. You can add to this list as you progress throughout therapy.

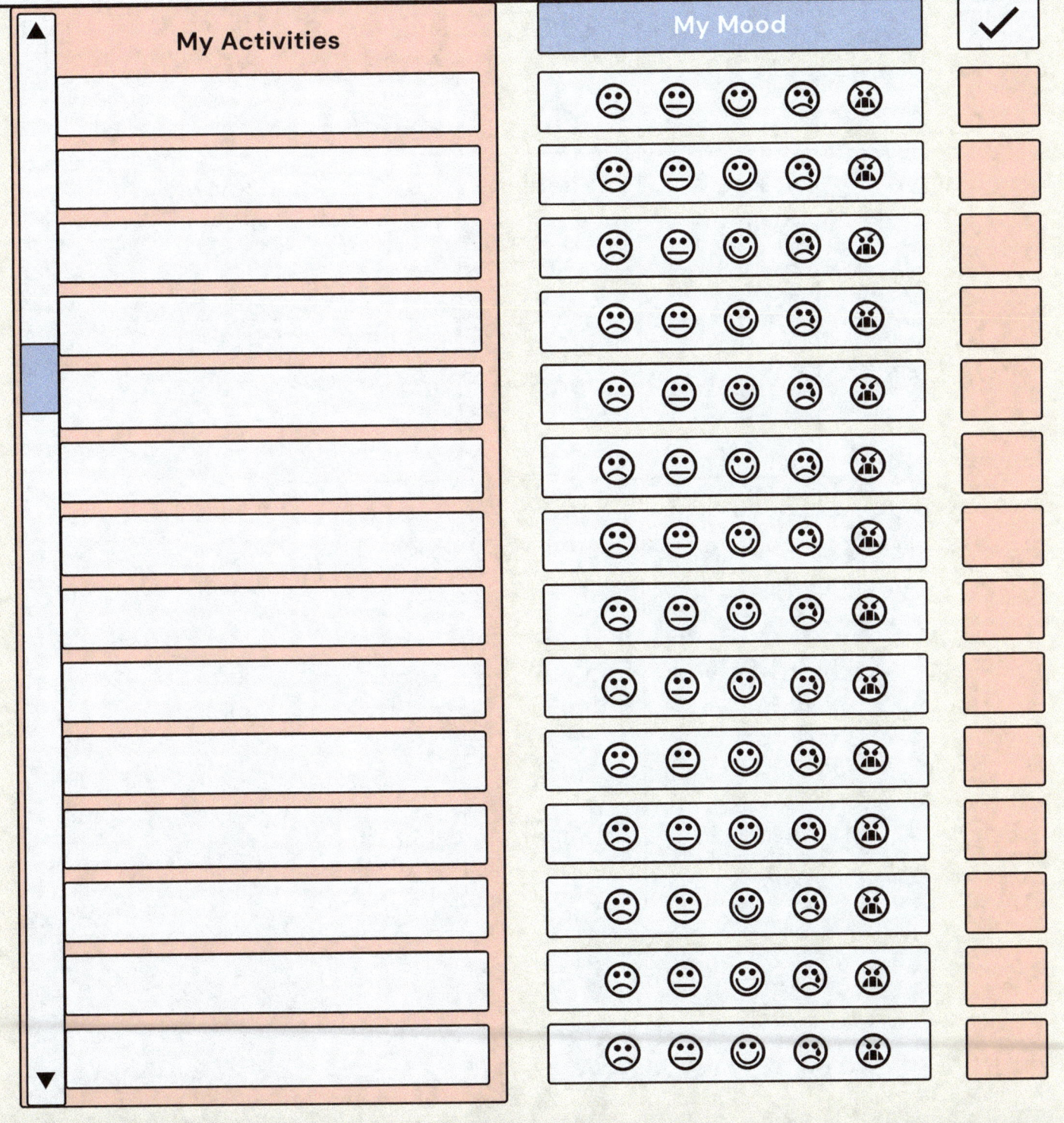

30-Day Self Care Challenge

Your healing journey REQUIRES your self-care. Challenge yourself to find new ways care for yourself especially while you are participating in the therapy process. Repe this challenge as often as needed. Notice the changes you experience.

Month: Year:

Write a letter	Go for a walk	Practice yoga	Light a candle	Take a nap
Go to bed earlier	Create a boundary	Eat healthy food	Watch a movie	Play with a pet
Pamper yourself	Go on a solo date	Practice gratitude	Try a DIY project	Ask for a hug
Speak up for yourself	Spend time in nature	Write a journal	Read a book	Watch the sunrise
Sit in the sun	Start a new hobby	Spa day at home	Grow a plant	Clean up your space
Eat mindfully	Learn a new skill	Set small goals	Drink plenty of water	Dance

Self Assessment

How do I feel at this moment?

What do I need and from who?

Overall Well-being
Yes | No

I get enough sleep
Yes | No

I spend time to recharge
Yes | No

I have a healthy eating habit
Yes | No

I keep my space clean
Yes | No

I exercise my body regularly
Yes | No

I take care of my hygiene
Yes | No

Self Reflection

> Taking care of yourself is the first step to taking care of others.
> -Bryant McGill

What keeps me grounded?

Who gives me comfort?

Where do I feel safest?

When am I at my best?

Free Flow Journal

As you reflect on your stated treatment goals and the progress you've made over the last weeks would you like things to be different? Are there additional barriers preventing you? What needs to happen to overcome these barriers? What creative ways can you contribute to your success?

Week 1
self check-in

DATE

THE GOOD BAD AND
UGLY OF THE WEEK

UPDATES I NEED TO MENTION: (IE:
MEDICATION, MEDICAL,
EXPERIENCES). DID I ADDRESS MY
ACTION STEPS THIS WEEK?
WHY/WHY NOT?

MOOD

This week in my session I need help with:

Week 1 After Therapy Dump

What we discussed

-
-
-
-

My Action Steps

Session Takeaways

MOOD

Week 2
self check-in

_____

DATE

_____

THE GOOD BAD AND
UGLY OF THE WEEK

UPDATES I NEED TO MENTION: (IE:
MEDICATION, MEDICAL,
EXPERIENCES). DID I ADDRESS MY
ACTION STEPS THIS WEEK?
WHY/WHY NOT?

MOOD

This week in my session I need help with:

Week 2 After Therapy Dump

What we discussed

-
-
-
-

My Action Steps

Session Takeaways

MOOD

Week 3
self check-in

DATE

THE GOOD BAD AND
UGLY OF THE WEEK

UPDATES I NEED TO MENTION: (IE:
MEDICATION, MEDICAL,
EXPERIENCES). DID I ADDRESS MY
ACTION STEPS THIS WEEK?
WHY/WHY NOT?

MOOD

This week in my session I need help with:

Week 3 After Therapy Dump

What we discussed

-
-
-
-

My Action Steps

Session Takeaways

MOOD

Week 4
self check-in

DATE

THE GOOD BAD AND
UGLY OF THE WEEK

UPDATES I NEED TO MENTION: (IE:
MEDICATION, MEDICAL,
EXPERIENCES). DID I ADDRESS MY
ACTION STEPS THIS WEEK?
WHY/WHY NOT?

MOOD

This week in my session I need help with:

Week 4 After Therapy Dump

What we discussed

-
-
-
-

My Action Steps

Session Takeaways

MOOD

My Goals List
MONTH 2

MONTH TWO DATE:

GOAL 1

GOAL 2

GOAL 3

ACTIONS I NEED TO TAKE

ACTIONS I NEED TO TAKE

ACTIONS I NEED TO TAKE

MONTHLY PROGRESS

MONTHLY PROGRESS

MONTHLY PROGRESS

NOTES

Self Assessment

Month Two

How do I feel at this moment?

What do I need and from who?

Overall Well-being

Yes | No

I get enough sleep

Yes | No

I spend time to recharge

Yes | No

I have a healthy eating habit

Yes | No

I keep my space clean

Yes | No

I exercise my body regularly

Yes | No

I take care of my hygiene

Yes | No

Self Reflection

Am I using my time wisely?

Am I taking anything for granted?

Am I employing a healthy perspective?

Am I living true to myself?

Free Flow Journal

As you reflect on your stated treatment goals and the progress you've made over the last month would you like things to be different? Are there additional barriers preventing you? What needs to happen to overcome these barriers? What creative ways can you contribute to your success?

Week 1
self check-in

_____

DATE

_____

THE GOOD BAD AND
UGLY OF THE WEEK

UPDATES I NEED TO MENTION: (IE:
MEDICATION, MEDICAL,
EXPERIENCES). DID I ADDRESS MY
ACTION STEPS THIS WEEK?
WHY/WHY NOT?

MOOD

This week in my session I need help with:

Week 1 After Therapy Dump

What we discussed

- ○
- ○
- ○
- ○

My Action Steps

Session Takeaways

MOOD

Week 2
self check-in

DATE

THE GOOD BAD AND
UGLY OF THE WEEK

UPDATES I NEED TO MENTION: (IE:
MEDICATION, MEDICAL,
EXPERIENCES). DID I ADDRESS MY
ACTION STEPS THIS WEEK?
WHY/WHY NOT?

MOOD

This week in my session I need help with:

Week 2 After Therapy Dump

What we discussed

-
-
-
-

My Action Steps

Session Takeaways

MOOD

Week 3
self check-in

DATE

THE GOOD BAD AND UGLY OF THE WEEK

UPDATES I NEED TO MENTION: (IE: MEDICATION, MEDICAL, EXPERIENCES). DID I ADDRESS MY ACTION STEPS THIS WEEK? WHY/WHY NOT?

MOOD

This week in my session I need help with:

Week 3 After Therapy Dump

What we discussed

-
-
-
-

My Action Steps

Session Takeaways

MOOD

Week 4
self check-in

DATE

THE GOOD BAD AND
UGLY OF THE WEEK

UPDATES I NEED TO MENTION: (IE:
MEDICATION, MEDICAL,
EXPERIENCES). DID I ADDRESS MY
ACTION STEPS THIS WEEK?
WHY/WHY NOT?

MOOD

This week in my session I need help with:

Week 4 After Therapy Dump

What we discussed

-
-
-
-

My Action Steps

Session Takeaways

MOOD

MONTH 3

MONTH THREE DATE:

GOAL 1	GOAL 2	GOAL 3

ACTIONS I NEED TO TAKE	ACTIONS I NEED TO TAKE	ACTIONS I NEED TO TAKE

MONTHLY PROGRESS	MONTHLY PROGRESS	MONTHLY PROGRESS

NOTES

Self Assessment

Month Three

How do I feel at this moment?

What do I need and from who?

Overall Well-being

| Yes | No |

I get enough sleep

| Yes | No |

I spend time to recharge

| Yes | No |

I have a healthy eating habit

| Yes | No |

I keep my space clean

| Yes | No |

I exercise my body regularly

| Yes | No |

I take care of my hygiene

| Yes | No |

Self Reflection

> Self-Care is how you take your power back.
> -Lalah Delia

Who am I, really?

What worries me most about the future?

If this were the last day of my life, would I have the same plans for today?

What am I really scared of?

Free Flow Journal

As you reflect on your stated treatment goals and the progress you've made over the last month would you like things to be different? Are there additional barriers preventing you? What needs to happen to overcome these barriers? What creative ways can you contribute to your success?

Week 1
self check-in

DATE

THE GOOD BAD AND
UGLY OF THE WEEK

UPDATES I NEED TO MENTION: (IE:
MEDICATION, MEDICAL,
EXPERIENCES). DID I ADDRESS MY
ACTION STEPS THIS WEEK?
WHY/WHY NOT?

MOOD

This week in my session I need help with:

Week 1 After Therapy Dump

What we discussed

-
-
-
-

My Action Steps

Session Takeaways

MOOD

Week 2
self check-in

DATE

THE GOOD BAD AND
UGLY OF THE WEEK

UPDATES I NEED TO MENTION: (IE:
MEDICATION, MEDICAL,
EXPERIENCES). DID I ADDRESS MY
ACTION STEPS THIS WEEK?
WHY/WHY NOT?

MOOD

This week in my session I need help with:

Week 2 After Therapy Dump

What we discussed

-
-
-
-

My Action Steps

Session Takeaways

MOOD

Week 3

self check-in

_____
DATE
_____

THE GOOD BAD AND UGLY OF THE WEEK

UPDATES I NEED TO MENTION: (IE: MEDICATION, MEDICAL, EXPERIENCES). DID I ADDRESS MY ACTION STEPS THIS WEEK? WHY/WHY NOT?

MOOD

This week in my session I need help with:

Week 3 After Therapy Dump

What we discussed

-
-
-
-

My Action Steps

Session Takeaways

MOOD

Week 4
self check-in

_____

DATE

_____

THE GOOD BAD AND
UGLY OF THE WEEK

UPDATES I NEED TO MENTION: (IE:
MEDICATION, MEDICAL,
EXPERIENCES). DID I ADDRESS MY
ACTION STEPS THIS WEEK?
WHY/WHY NOT?

MOOD

This week in my session I need help with:

Week 4 After Therapy Dump

What we discussed

-
-
-
-

My Action Steps

Session Takeaways

MOOD

My Goals List
MONTH 4

MONTH FOUR DATE:

GOAL 1

GOAL 2

GOAL 3

ACTIONS I NEED TO TAKE

ACTIONS I NEED TO TAKE

ACTIONS I NEED TO TAKE

MONTHLY PROGRESS

MONTHLY PROGRESS

MONTHLY PROGRESS

 NOTES

Self Assessment

Month Four

How do I feel at this moment?

What do I need and from who?

Overall Well-being

Yes   No

I get enough sleep

Yes   No

I spend time to recharge

Yes   No

I have a healthy eating habit

Yes   No

I keep my space clean

Yes   No

I exercise my body regularly

Yes   No

I take care of my hygiene

Yes   No

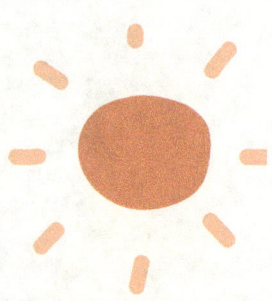

Self Reflection

> It's not selfish to love yourself, take care of yourself, and to make your happiness a priority. It's necessary
> -Mandy Hale

Am I holding on to something I need to let go of?

What matters most in my life?

Why do I matter?

What have I given up on?

Free Flow Journal

As you reflect on your stated treatment goals and the progress you've made over the last month would you like things to be different? Are there additional barriers preventing you? What needs to happen to overcome these barriers? What creative ways can you contribute to your success?

Week 1
self check-in

DATE

THE GOOD BAD AND
UGLY OF THE WEEK

UPDATES I NEED TO MENTION: (IE:
MEDICATION, MEDICAL,
EXPERIENCES). DID I ADDRESS MY
ACTION STEPS THIS WEEK?
WHY/WHY NOT?

MOOD

This week in my session I need help with:

Week 1 After Therapy Dump

What we discussed

-
-
-
-

My Action Steps

Session Takeaways

MOOD

Week 2
self check-in

DATE

THE GOOD BAD AND
UGLY OF THE WEEK

UPDATES I NEED TO MENTION: (IE:
MEDICATION, MEDICAL,
EXPERIENCES). DID I ADDRESS MY
ACTION STEPS THIS WEEK?
WHY/WHY NOT?

MOOD

This week in my session I need help with:

Week 2 After Therapy Dump

What we discussed

-
-
-
-

My Action Steps

Session Takeaways

MOOD

Week 3
self check-in

_____

DATE

_____

THE GOOD BAD AND
UGLY OF THE WEEK

UPDATES I NEED TO MENTION: (IE: MEDICATION, MEDICAL, EXPERIENCES). DID I ADDRESS MY ACTION STEPS THIS WEEK? WHY/WHY NOT?

MOOD

This week in my session I need help with:

Week 3 After Therapy Dump

What we discussed

-
-
-
-

My Action Steps

Session Takeaways

MOOD

Week 4
self check-in

DATE

THE GOOD BAD AND
UGLY OF THE WEEK

UPDATES I NEED TO MENTION: (IE:
MEDICATION, MEDICAL,
EXPERIENCES). DID I ADDRESS MY
ACTION STEPS THIS WEEK?
WHY/WHY NOT?

MOOD

This week in my session I need help with:

Week 4 After Therapy Dump

What we discussed

-
-
-
-

My Action Steps

Session Takeaways

MOOD

My Goals List
MONTH 5

MONTH FIVE DATE:

GOAL 1	GOAL 2	GOAL 3

ACTIONS I NEED TO TAKE	ACTIONS I NEED TO TAKE	ACTIONS I NEED TO TAKE

MONTHLY PROGRESS	MONTHLY PROGRESS	MONTHLY PROGRESS

NOTES

Self Assessment

Month Five

How do I feel at this moment?

What do I need and from who?

Overall Well-being

Yes | No

I get enough sleep

Yes | No

I spend time to recharge

Yes | No

I have a healthy eating habit

Yes | No

I keep my space clean

Yes | No

I exercise my body regularly

Yes | No

I take care of my hygiene

Yes | No

Self Reflection

> **Self-Care is not self-indulgence; it is self-preservation.**
> -Audre Lorde

When did I last push the boundaries of my comfort zone?

What do I need to change about myself?

Who has had the greatest impact on my life?

What is life asking of me?

Free Flow Journal

As you reflect on your stated treatment goals and the progress you've made over the last month would you like things to be different? Are there additional barriers preventing you? What needs to happen to overcome these barriers? What creative ways can you contribute to your success?

Week 1
self check-in

DATE

THE GOOD BAD AND
UGLY OF THE WEEK

UPDATES I NEED TO MENTION: (IE:
MEDICATION, MEDICAL,
EXPERIENCES). DID I ADDRESS MY
ACTION STEPS THIS WEEK?
WHY/WHY NOT?

MOOD

This week in my session I need help with:

Week 1 After Therapy Dump

What we discussed

-
-
-
-

My Action Steps

Session Takeaways

MOOD

Week 2
self check-in

_____

DATE

_____

THE GOOD BAD AND
UGLY OF THE WEEK

UPDATES I NEED TO MENTION: (IE:
MEDICATION, MEDICAL,
EXPERIENCES). DID I ADDRESS MY
ACTION STEPS THIS WEEK?
WHY/WHY NOT?

MOOD

This week in my session I need help with:

Week 2 After Therapy Dump

What we discussed

My Action Steps

Session Takeaways

MOOD

Week 3
self check-in

_____

DATE

_____

THE GOOD BAD AND UGLY OF THE WEEK

UPDATES I NEED TO MENTION: (IE: MEDICATION, MEDICAL, EXPERIENCES). DID I ADDRESS MY ACTION STEPS THIS WEEK? WHY/WHY NOT?

MOOD

This week in my session I need help with:

Week 3 After Therapy Dump

What we discussed

-
-
-
-

My Action Steps

Session Takeaways

MOOD

Week 4
self check-in

DATE

THE GOOD BAD AND
UGLY OF THE WEEK

UPDATES I NEED TO MENTION: (IE:
MEDICATION, MEDICAL,
EXPERIENCES). DID I ADDRESS MY
ACTION STEPS THIS WEEK?
WHY/WHY NOT?

MOOD

This week in my session I need help with:

Week 4 After Therapy Dump

What we discussed

-
-
-
-

My Action Steps

Session Takeaways

MOOD

Self Assessment

Month Six

How do I feel at this moment?

What do I need and from who?

Overall Well-being
Yes   No

I get enough sleep
Yes   No

I spend time to recharge
Yes   No

I have a healthy eating habit
Yes   No

I keep my space clean
Yes   No

I exercise my body regularly
Yes   No

I take care of my hygiene
Yes   No

Self Reflection

> **Be enough for yourself. The rest of the world can wait.**
> -Unknown

The words I'd like to live by are . . .

I couldn't imagine living without . . .

What does unconditional love look like?

really wish others knew this about me . . .

Free Flow Journal

As you reflect on your stated treatment goals and the progress you've made over the last month would you like things to be different? Are there additional barriers preventing you? What needs to happen to overcome these barriers? What creative ways can you contribute to your success?

My Goals List

MONTH 6

MONTH SIX DATE:

GOAL1	GOAL 2	GOAL 3

ACTIONS I NEED TO TAKE	ACTIONS I NEED TO TAKE	ACTIONS I NEED TO TAKE

MONTHLY PROGRESS	MONTHLY PROGRESS	MONTHLY PROGRESS

NOTES

Week 1
self check-in

DATE

THE GOOD BAD AND
UGLY OF THE WEEK

UPDATES I NEED TO MENTION: (IE:
MEDICATION, MEDICAL,
EXPERIENCES). DID I ADDRESS MY
ACTION STEPS THIS WEEK?
WHY/WHY NOT?

MOOD

This week in my session I need help with:

Week 1 After Therapy Dump

What we discussed

-
-
-
-

My Action Steps

Session Takeaways

MOOD

Week 2
self check-in

_____

DATE

_____

**THE GOOD BAD AND
UGLY OF THE WEEK**

UPDATES I NEED TO MENTION: (IE:
MEDICATION, MEDICAL,
EXPERIENCES). DID I ADDRESS MY
ACTION STEPS THIS WEEK?
WHY/WHY NOT?

MOOD

This week in my session I need help with:

Week 2 After Therapy Dump

What we discussed

- ●
- ●
- ●
- ●

My Action Steps

Session Takeaways

MOOD

Week 3
self check-in

DATE

THE GOOD BAD AND
UGLY OF THE WEEK

UPDATES I NEED TO MENTION: (IE:
MEDICATION, MEDICAL,
EXPERIENCES). DID I ADDRESS MY
ACTION STEPS THIS WEEK?
WHY/WHY NOT?

MOOD

This week in my session I need help with:

Week 3 After Therapy Dump

What we discussed

-
-
-
-

My Action Steps

Session Takeaways

MOOD

Week 4
self check-in

_____

DATE

_____

THE GOOD BAD AND
UGLY OF THE WEEK

UPDATES I NEED TO MENTION: (IE:
MEDICATION, MEDICAL,
EXPERIENCES). DID I ADDRESS MY
ACTION STEPS THIS WEEK?
WHY/WHY NOT?

MOOD

This week in my session I need help with:

Week 4 After Therapy Dump

What we discussed

-
-
-
-

My Action Steps

Session Takeaways

MOOD

STAGE FOUR
Discharge
& AFTERCARE

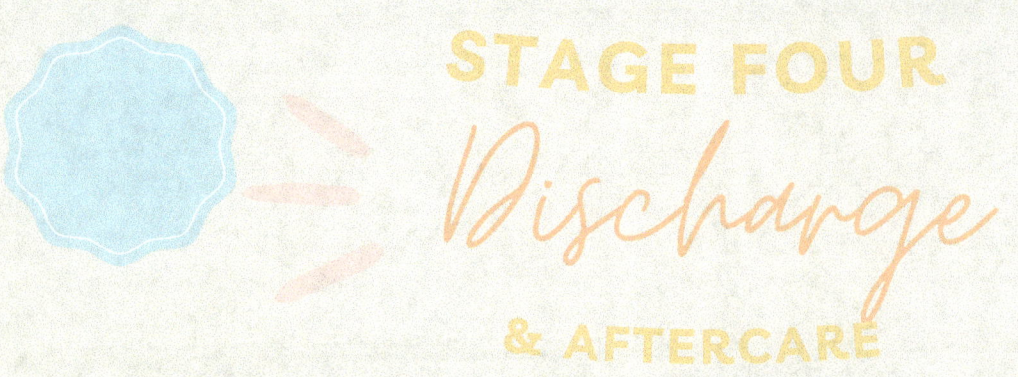

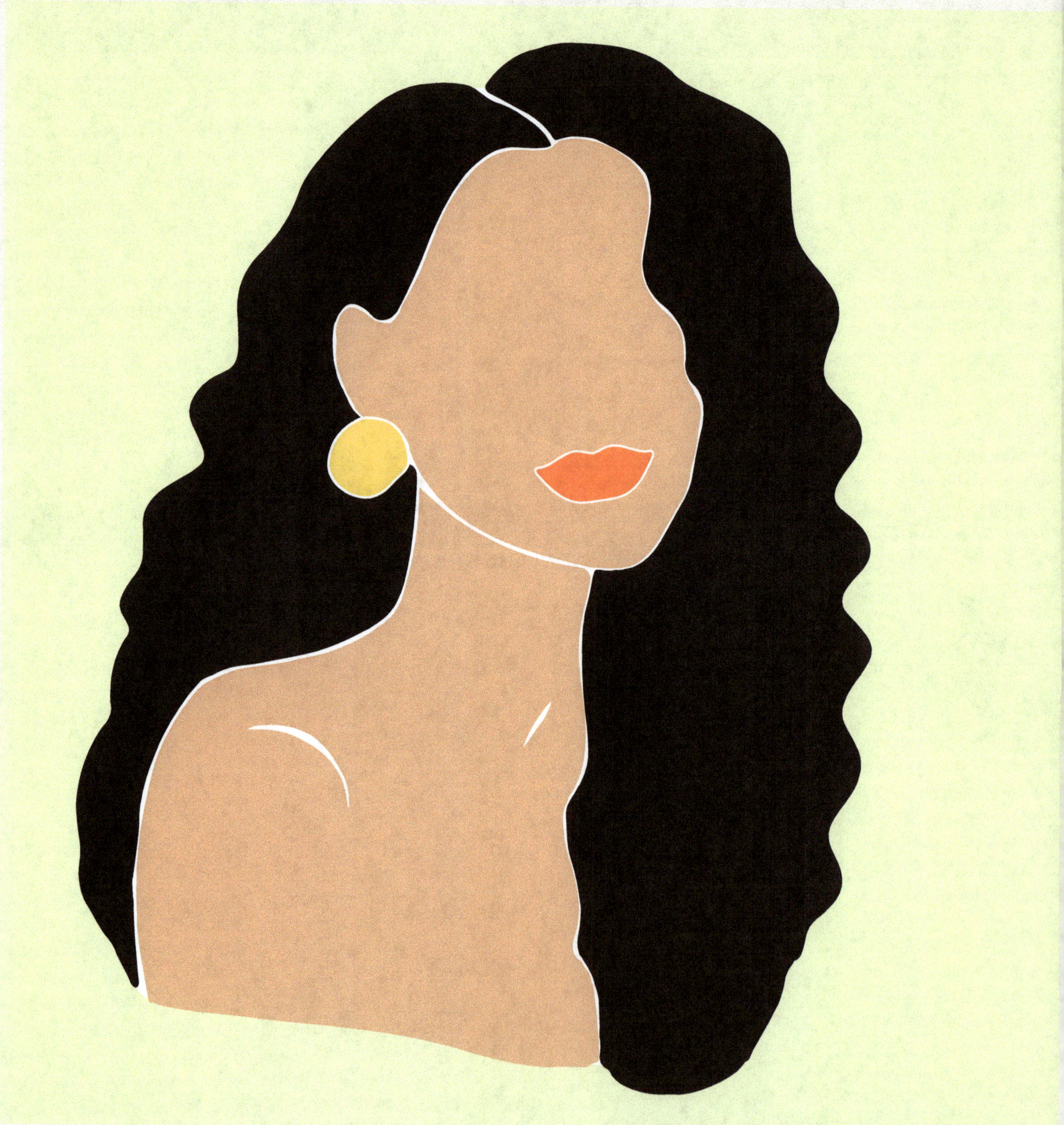

Dear
DIARY

Welcome to the final stage of your healing journey. You have accomplished the huge tasks of rocking your therapy goals. The work is not finished-it is life long therefore this stage is about setting yourself up for long term success. Today, journal your thoughts regarding the process.

Discharge PREPARATION

Discharge when...

○ You've maintained a significant reduction in symptoms or issues related to their presenting problem.

○ Your remaining problems are better treated by other means (e.g. medication management or a support group).

○ You've been in treatment for a considerable amount of time and have become stagnant with your progress.

○ You've developed skills you are now able to apply to new problem areas.

Things you should know

Final Diagnosis

_____

_____

_____

Prescribed Medication

_____

_____

_____

How will you maintain your healing after discharge?

THERAPY SUMMARY

Date: Month: Year:

I AM PROUD OF:

HOW I ACCOMPLISHED MY GOALS:

I THOUGHT I WOULD NEVER:

I WANT TO CONTINUE WORKING ON:

Care Plan

HOW DO I KNOW WHEN I NEED HELP?

MY COPING SKILLS

NAME & CONTACTS OF MY SUPPORTS

What I will do in emergencies

Free Flow Journal

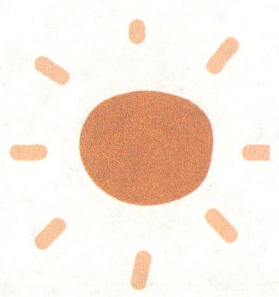

Free Flow Journal

Free Flow Journal

Free Flow Journal

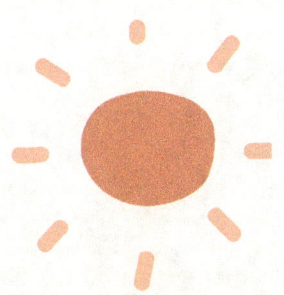

Free Flow Journal

Free Flow Journal